Original title:
Cedar Secrets

Copyright © 2025 Creative Arts Management OÜ
All rights reserved.

Author: Aidan Marlowe
ISBN HARDBACK: 978-1-80567-226-5
ISBN PAPERBACK: 978-1-80567-525-9

The Lore of Leaf and Limb

In the forest where shadows play,
The branches gossip every day.
Squirrels with secrets, oh what a sight!
Chattering critters steal the night.

The trees tell tales, oh so absurd,
Of acorns that twirl and nuts that stirred.
A raccoon with style, a badger with flair,
They prance and dance without a care.

Woodpeckers tap a comedic beat,
As owls bust jokes—they can't be beat!
The wind laughs softly, gives a nudge,
While pine cones roll, refusing to budge.

In this world where laughter thrives,
The leaves shake hands, the laughter arrives.
Join the fun, let worries release,
Nature's a party, a joyful piece!

Echoes of Silent Growth

In the forest, whispers play,
Tall trees giggle, night and day.
Their shadows dance with silly flair,
Roots tell jokes, if you dare!

Leaves that Hold the Past

Old leaves chuckle, making plans,
Telling tales with little hands.
They gossip about the wind's last spin,
And laugh at squirrels, wild and thin.

A Canopy of Mystery

Under branches, secrets twirl,
Tree trunks twist, and ribbons swirl.
Creatures peek with curious eyes,
While shadows dodge beneath the skies.

The Heartbeat of Green Giants

Big trees thud, a rhythmic beat,
As critters dance on nimble feet.
Leaves clap hands, a leafy cheer,
Join the party, bring your beer!

Shadows of the Evergreen

Beneath the boughs, the squirrels prance,
Hiding nuts with a crafty glance.
A squirrel stole my sandwich wrap,
In a game of epic woodland cap!

The owls gossip in the night,
Recalling tales of feathered flight.
Grumpy raccoons look out of tune,
As racquets clash beneath the moon.

The Tree's Hidden Tales

Whispers rustle through each leaf,
The stories somehow bring me grief.
An ant insists it saw a moose,
While beetles dance with gentle juice.

The branches giggle with each breeze,
While birds try to play hide and tease.
A bear gives a very loud yawn,
As gossip spreads upon the lawn.

Scent of the Old Wood

I wandered deep where nothing's neat,
And tripped on roots, oh what a feat!
The fresh pine smell was quite a treat,
But fell, my face met dirt's warm seat!

The woodpecker pecks with no shame,
Assuming I'm part of his game.
The sap drips down with giggles loud,
As nature forms its silly crowd.

Bark and Breath

The trees hold secrets in their rings,
Of all the laughter that living brings.
A branch once thought it could break dance,
But only managed a silly prance.

While saplings stretch to reach the sun,
A twig claims it can outdo the fun.
With every breeze, my troubles flee,
As nature winks, just wait and see!

Secrets of the Coniferous

In a forest where whispers dwell,
Trees share tales they won't tell.
A squirrel with a gossip spree,
Eavesdrops on each coniferous glee.

The pine needles chuckle, oh so sly,
As the branches dance under the sky.
"Did you hear what the oak tree said?"
"He's gone bald! Now he's full of dread!"

Roots That Remember

Beneath the ground, where roots intertwine,
Old legends grow like ancient wine.
One root whispers, "I knew that guy,"
Another chuckles, "Oh, me? Just shy!"

They gossip of storms and sunlit days,
Of fallen leaves and love's silly ways.
"Remember that time we dug too deep?"
"Oh yes, that laugh still makes me weep!"

Beneath the Canopy's Veil

Under leaves like a green-draped stage,
The forest laughs, it's all the rage.
A fox in a hat, he'd just arrived,
Said, "This party's where we all thrive!"

The ferns throw shade, play cards with glee,
While the owls hoot a tune, carefree.
"Who's got the acorns? Let's make a snack!"
"Just mind the squirrels, they'll raid the pack!"

Stories in the Sap

The sap drips slowly, a sticky delight,
Each drop a story, day turns to night.
"Oh darling, that one's from spring's bright bloom!"
"Then why does it smell like old vacuum?"

The bugs join in with hilarious flair,
"Remember that time when we lost our hair?"
It's a sticky situation, laughter all around,
In the syrupy tales where humor is found.

The Twilight Fable of Wood and Sky

In the twilight, trees do dance,
With rustling leaves, they take a chance.
Squirrels giggle, birds join too,
As branches twist, and shadows grew.

A whisper floats through branches high,
Telling tales of the shy butterfly.
The woodpecker plays a rhythmic beat,
While owls wink in their night retreat.

Murmurs in the Mossy Mold

Beneath the canopy, whispers bloom,
Frogs croak loud, creating a boom.
Mossy patches hide critters small,
Joking around, they have a ball.

The snail shouts, 'I'm winning the race!'
While the turtle claims, 'I'll set the pace.'
Laughter echoes, surrounded by green,
Nature's jesters, in a playful scene.

Painted Layers of Time

Layers whisper of colors bright,
Rust and green in the fading light.
An old log chuckles, 'Look at my age!'
While fungi giggle, stealing the stage.

Bees buzz by, with puns aplenty,
Creating a buzz that's quite trendy.
Each brush of time, a ticklish tease,
Carved by the sun and the playful breeze.

The Lullaby of Living Grain

Winds sing softly, a grainy tune,
Tickling stalks beneath the moon.
The dandelion puffs a gentle jest,
"Catch me if you can, I'm the best!"

The corn cob whispered sweet secrets low,
As rabbits pranced, putting on a show.
Fields of laughter sway and beam,
In the lullaby of a grainy dream.

Pondering the Timber's Time

In the wood, trees make a fuss,
Squirrels arguing, making a bus.
Time ticks by, branches sway,
Who knew trees could be such cliché?

Birds chat gossip in the breeze,
Telling tales with such expertise.
'Did you hear about the fallen sprout?'
Trees can't help but laugh out loud.

Roots are tangled, a secret knot,
Whispers in the forest, what a plot!
Every year they shed their leaves,
But juicy tales are what it weaves.

Sun-drenched days stretch out their arms,
While shadows giggle, spreading charms.
Timber's wisdom, so absurd,
Who knew silence could be heard?

Solace in the Sap

When the sun drips down like honey,
Trees chill out, they think it's funny.
Sap oozes slowly with sticky delight,
And bugs flock in for a sweet bite.

Sticky fingers, what a mess,
Crafting treasures, nonetheless.
The more they gather, the more they laugh,
Nature's candy, a quirky craft.

Branches shaking, having a ball,
Nature's humor, it charms us all.
Saplings giggle at the mighty trunks,
Rooted deep in their playful funks.

So next time you wander through trees,
Listen closely to their giddy pleas.
For in the sap, joy is trapped,
Just make sure you don't get sapped!

The Sentinel's Shelter

Underneath the leafy watch,
A fearless sapling takes a swatch.
Guarding secrets, standing proud,
Echoing whispers, oh so loud.

The sentinel stands with a grin,
All the tales that lie within.
It cackles low, as shadows creep,
Watching rivals talk in sleep.

In the glen where no one looks,
Nature's gossip fills the books.
Every crack and every twist,
Hides a tale that can't be missed.

As night unfolds, they share a laugh,
The old bark shares a silly schism.
Sentinel grins, "Come take a seat,
Nature's laughter is quite the treat!"

Buried Dreams in the Bark's Embrace

Beneath the bark are dreams untold,
Little wishes, bright and bold.
Knots and scars, with stories sewn,
In nature's plot, they've all grown.

A tree might say, in leafy tones,
"It's not just roots that fill my bones."
Each ring a chapter, who would guess?
How a tree can knit such mess!

Whispers echo, like giddy chimes,
Raccoons plotting in funny rhymes.
Digging deep where hopes take flight,
Nature's quirk is pure delight.

So next time you find a tree,
Listen closely, what might it be?
With dreams and laughter intertwined,
In bark's embrace, joy's defined!

The Spirit Within the Bough

In the branches up so high,
A squirrel's plotting with a sigh.
"What if I wore a tiny hat?"
He chuckles soft, imagining that.

The wise old owl rolls his eyes,
"You'll scare the birds, oh what a surprise!"
But laughter dances in the leaves,
As nature spins tales that never deceives.

Echoes Beneath the Stars

When the moon peeks through the pine,
A raccoon sings, feeling divine.
He twirls around, quite out of tune,
While shadows join in the muffled croon.

The fireflies blink in pure delight,
"This dance party's a true highlight!"
With twinkling eyes, they twirl and sway,
Adding glow to the fun-filled play.

Trails of the Tall Trees

A trail of ants, in a line so neat,
Refuse to admit defeat with their feat.
"We're on a mission to find some cheese!"
They boast with pride, swaying in the breeze.

A fox nearby, with a sly little grin,
Says, "Good luck, but watch for the bin!"
And the ants shudder but carry on,
Dreaming of cheese while dusk turns to dawn.

A Biography of Bark

Bark, a wise old fellow indeed,
With stories buried deep like a seed.
"I've seen the ages, the storms and the sun,
And let me tell ya, it's all been fun!"

He scratches his grooves and starts to narrate,
About a time that was simply first-rate.
"A raccoon once mistook me for a lunch,
But he soon learned I'm not a leafy munch!"

Nostalgia in the Needle-Laden Breeze

In a forest where laughter echoes bright,
Hidden tales dance in the soft moonlight.
A squirrel on a branch, wearing a crown,
Sings of the days when no one wore a frown.

Mossy carpets and whispers so clear,
Tickling the secrets that trees hold dear.
Uncle Pine's jokes, oh, how they would flow,
While Aunt Spruce rolled her eyes, stealing the show.

Twilight's Bark-bound Mysteries

Beneath tangled branches, a laughter does swell,
Bark-scratchers telling their tales quite well.
The shadows play tag in the dusky hour,
While owls share gossip from their lofty tower.

One tree tells of a lost acorn's quest,
While another insists it once wore a vest.
The moon chuckles softly, a bead of delight,
As whispers of twilight add spice to the night.

Roots that Remember

In the soil where stories intertwine,
Roots gossip about the old woodland line.
With each twist and turn of the ancient base,
They share silly secrets in their cozy space.

A rumor of a wild root-tango dance,
In the cool of the night, it took quite a chance.
With laughter and jiving, they swayed and spun,
While the mushrooms watched with such joy and fun.

The Conifer's Soliloquy

Greetings, dear creatures, come gather around,
For I've tales of joy just itching to sound.
With needles like quills, I pen down my jest,
Of chipmunks in bow ties, oh, they look their best!

A pinecone's adventure, all twisting and turning,
A dance of the sap, so delightfully burning.
With laughter so hearty, the forest will roar,
For each joke I share opens up woodland's door.

Cradle of the Wild

In the forest where squirrels play,
Frogs sing raps at the end of the day.
Leaves giggle with a rustling cheer,
Squirrels plotting without any fear.

Raccoons host parties with mushrooms galore,
While owls hoot jokes till we can't take more.
The moon beams down with a chuckling grin,
As the wild ones dance, let the fun begin!

Branches sway to the rhythm of delight,
Each creature shines under starlit night.
Nature's circus, it's truly a sight,
Where laughter and mischief take joyful flight.

So join the revel, let worries subside,
In the cradle where wild spirits abide.
For even the trees have a soft chuckle too,
In this land where the innocent have fun to pursue.

Tangles of Time

In a tangle where the old tales unwind,
A snail thinks he's the fastest, oh, what a find!
Rabbits giggle as they hop about,
While wise old owls say, 'Don't knock it out!'

The wind carries laughter from branch to root,
As foxes strut in their fanciest suit.
Every twist and turn hides a playful find,
Time tricks us all, oh, isn't it blind?

Tangled paths lead to a jesters' parade,
Where shadows play games and never do fade.
Each corner holds secrets and silly surprise,
As time tangles up in the forest of lies.

So wander through whims, let your heart be light,
In the jigsaw of joy that stretches so bright.
For every misstep is a laugh to embrace,
In this funny old world, it's a magical place.

Wisdom in the Wild Wood

A grumpy old badger, wise and astute,
Turns to a rabbit and says, 'You're too cute!'
The trees lean in, they can't help but eavesdrop,
As critters form circles, giggling nonstop.

'What's the secret to a life full of cheer?'
The wise badger chuckles and says, 'Bring your beer!'
Pine cones clap as the forest giggles loud,
Wisdom comes wrapped in the silliest shroud.

With every tall tale under the old oaks,
Foxes share laughter and skits with sweet jokes.
It's hard to be serious when fun's on display,
In the wild wood, laughter's the only way.

So dance with the shadows, let giggles be heard,
For wisdom is found in the humor of birds.
In the heart of the wild, where secrets entwine,
Laughter and wisdom together align.

Whispers of the Old Ones

The old trees whisper with a chuckle and sway,
'Things are not always what they seem, we say!'
Little mice scamper, with gleams in their eyes,
As branches bend down to share all their lies.

A bear tries yoga, but stumbles and rolls,
While birds gossip softly, exchanging their roles.
'This tree can dance!' claims a squirrel with glee,
'But only when no one happens to see!'

With each rustling leaf, secrets drift on by,
As the laughter of old ones fills up the sky.
In this kooky old world where wisdom takes flight,
The fun never ends, even deep in the night.

So heed the calls and let your spirit fly,
Join the whispers of old ones, don't be shy.
For in every giggle and chuckle that flows,
Lies the heart of the forest, where true laughter grows.

The Embrace of Soil and Sky

The trees hold up their limbs so high,
As if they're reaching for the pie.
With roots that dance and sway below,
They whisper tales we long to know.

In muddy shoes, we stomp around,
And giggle at the silly sound.
The branches tickle our upturned noses,
We dodge and weave like silly roses.

A squirrel darts past with quite the flair,
While mossy hats declare, "Who cares?"
The laughter echoes in the breeze,
As leaves laugh softly with the trees.

So here we sit in nature's clutches,
Sharing joy with all its touches.
The soil, the sky, a playful pair,
In this grand tale of trees laid bare.

Gnarled Memories

The knotted trunks hold tales untold,
Of squirrel thieves and acorn gold.
Each twist and turn, a memory steeped,
In laughter shared and secrets keeped.

A knot so big, it must be wise,
With tiny birds in feathered ties.
They chirp about the pranks they've played,
On passersby, who just dismayed.

A spider spins with crafty cheer,
Insisting that it's not what you hear.
While gnarled limbs shake in pure delight,
The sun sets down, a golden light.

So gather 'round the twisted bark,
And listen closely to the lark.
For every bend tells a funny tale,
Of windy days and autumn's gale.

The Secret Song of Roots

Below the surface, they wiggle and spin,
A secret dance where all begin.
They sing of mud and hidden joys,
Of ancient games with earthy toys.

With tippy toes, the grass does sway,
They tease the beetles in their play.
The roots hum tunes of comical tales,
Of mischief stirred in summer gales.

While worms conduct a concert grand,
With tiny hats and a wooden band.
Each rustling leaf joins the rhyme,
As roots revel in their fun time.

So next you walk in the forest deep,
And feel the earth beneath your feet,
Just halt and listen, you won't ignore,
The laughter echoing from the floor.

In the Company of Trees

Oh, the trees are such jokesters, oh so spry,
With branches full of high-flying pie!
They giggle as the breezes dart,
And toss the leaves with a merry heart.

A wise old oak whispers 'Come sit tight,'
As I share my chips by firelight.
With pine cone hats and acorn crowns,
These leafy folks dance up and down.

The critters join in the funny fest,
With squirrels and rabbits, oh what a quest!
Each laugh rings out like a royal decree,
In the playful arms of the leafy spree.

So grab your friends and join the fun,
When life gets dull, just look up—run!
For in the company of trees so wise,
You'll find your joy beneath the skies.

Shadows Dancing on Pine

In the woods where shadows play,
A squirrel wears a hat today,
He twirls and leaps with such finesse,
While branches giggle, what a mess!

The owls hoot, they clap their wings,
As mice perform their silly things,
The pine trees sway, they share a grin,
While acorns fall, let the fun begin!

The Forest's Fragile Diary

Upon the bark, the scribbles show,
A beaver writes, 'I'm quite the pro!'
With tiny paws and pencil near,
He chronicles the woodland cheer.

The deer debate on fashion trends,
While rabbits hop, they make amends,
Each leaf a page, the stories twine,
In nature's book, oh so divine!

Whispers in the Forest

The trees are gossiping today,
With rustling leaves, they have their say,
A chipmunk claims he saw a ghost,
While shadows giggle, and they boast!

The crickets chirp the latest news,
While fireflies dance in vibrant hues,
They wink and nod, a secret keep,
As night descends, the forest sleeps.

Beneath the Ancient Boughs

Beneath the boughs so grand and tall,
A raccoon hosts his yearly ball,
With jelly beans and berry pies,
Who knew the woods could be so spry?

The fox arrives in sparkly shoes,
While toadstools cheer, they share the news,
And all around, a joyous sound,
At midnight's feast, fun knows no bound!

Fragrance of Forgotten Paths

In the woods, a squirrel prances,
Chasing shadows, doing dances.
He thinks he's sly, but oh, the jest,
For all the birds know he's a pest.

With every nut, he plots and schemes,
While trees whisper their leafy dreams.
But what's that smell? A picnic spread!
Oh no, not again—more crumbs to dread!

Beneath the boughs, a hiker trips,
With tangled shoelaces and snack-filled lips.
The chipmunks laugh, they cheer and squeak,
While the hiker blushes, feeling weak.

So when you roam these funny thickets,
Beware the trees and their mean pickets.
For in their shade, adventure hides,
Along with giggles and leafy slides.

Wooded Enigmas Unveiled

Beneath the canopy so dense,
Lies a mystery so immense.
What's that rustle in the leaves?
A bear with socks, or just some thieves?

A gnome appears with a cheeky grin,
Sipping tea from a recycling bin.
He tells tall tales of forest lore,
While raccoons volunteer for the encore.

The owls hoot in fits of glee,
Playing games like hide and seek.
Each twig snapped is a laughter score,
As woodland creatures beg for more.

Morning light breaks with a chuckle,
The trees sway, they wiggle and shuffle.
In this realm of secret laughs,
Nature's riddle is a playful path.

Tales in the Twisting Trunks

In a clearing where sunlight dances,
Trees twist and loop in funny prances.
One trunk claims it's a mighty snake,
While the others laugh, "It's just a flake!"

A wise old oak, with wisdom wide,
Says he's tired, let the branches slide.
"Why stand tall when you can recline,
A life less serious is simply divine!"

Saplings gossip with branches low,
Dreaming of kingdoms they'll never grow.
They giggle and whisper, a sassy bunch,
Discussing their dreams over a light lunch.

As twilight paints the sky with glee,
The trees tell jokes to the bumblebee.
In the forest, where laughter runs,
Every twist and turn is full of puns.

Echoing the Wind's Lullaby

The wind sings softly through the leaves,
With whispers of mischief that it weaves.
Mocking the clouds that drift and sway,
  Telling them not to take life too gray.

Squirrels chirp, in unison they cheer,
While the moon winks, drawing near.
It joins the dance, a celestial muse,
Creating a riddle even the stars can't choose.

A friendly breeze, with a giggle or two,
Whirls around, making a cozy brew.
'Catch me if you can,' it seems to say,
While the trees bow down in playful dismay.

Every gust carries a tale untold,
Of woodland antics, brave and bold.
So close your eyes, let your worries fly,
  As nature giggles with a lullaby.

Secrets of the Timbered Heart

In the forest, trees have dreams,
Barking up their plans, it seems.
Whispers float on breezy nights,
A squirrel's tale of daring flights.

Leaves giggle as they sway along,
Moss joins in with a bouncing song.
Acorns chuckle from the ground,
While branches dance, they twist around.

Roots have gossip, tangled tight,
About the owls who hoot at night.
A raccoon in a hat so grand,
Steals the show, a nature band.

So when you stroll and hear their cheer,
Remember trees have tales, my dear.
With laughter woven into bark,
Their jokes beneath the moonlight spark.

Sapling's Silent Story

Little sapling stands so proud,
Whispering secrets, soft and loud.
What's that tickle? A passing breeze,
Or just the giggles of busy bees?

In the shade, a baby fern,
Cracks jokes but never learns.
While raindrops fall, the puddles form,
Reflecting all their leafy charm.

Blades of grass play hide and seek,
With sunlight glimmers, they peek-a-boo sneak.
The branches, too, join in for fun,
Chasing shadows 'til day is done.

A band of critters gather 'round,
They laugh at tales of the world they found.
In every rustle, in every part,
Lies a playful sapling's heart.

Echoes of the Forest Floor

Footsteps crunch on a carpeted floor,
With echoes of laughter, who could ask for more?
A family of ants starts to parade,
In tiny hats that they have made.

Mushrooms wiggle as they peek,
From shady spots where they can sneak.
A chorus of crickets sings with glee,
While butterflies dance, carefree and free.

The forest floor, a stage for all,
Where twigs and stones do lightly call.
As pinecones tumble, giggles rise,
From friendly critters in disguise.

The trees all lean in to hear the cheer,
As voices blend with nature's clear.
In whispers shared among the leaves,
The forest's laughter never leaves.

The Grove's Hidden Tales

Under branches, stories hide,
Of whispering winds and critters' pride.
Old logs chuckle with every turn,
While little roots share what they learn.

A shadow darts with a cheeky grin,
As woodland creatures join in the din.
Sap-soaked tales from barky chairs,
Declared by owls with ruffled airs.

In thickets thick, the chatter flows,
With playful jabs and funny prose.
The breeze is cheeky, nipping at toes,
As laughter blooms, where no one knows.

So if you wander the green delight,
Don't miss the tales woven in light.
For every step in the grove takes flight,
Is wrapped with joy, from day to night.

The Tapestry of Thickets

In the thicket where squirrels jest,
The bushes wear hats; they look their best.
Rabbits throw parties, all day long,
With carrots for snacks, they dance to a song.

The hedgehog is DJ; he spins with glee,
While foxes line up, sipping sweet tea.
A badger in stripes leads the conga line,
In this leafy ball, everything's fine!

Green foliage giggles, the sun peeks through,
The laughter of leaves, a bright morning hue.
Nature's own revelry, wild and spry,
Who knew thickets could throw such a sly high?

Each stem tells a tale, each twig has a grin,
Join the fun in the woods, where chaos begins!
In the heart of the thicket, the laughter won't cease,
A woodland ball in nature's own lease!

Silence at the Summit

At the summit, the view is grand,
But the squirrels are plotting, a nutty band.
With binoculars perched, they scout the plains,
For mischief and games in their tiny domains.

They whisper and giggle, under the pine,
A plan to outsmart the climbing feline.
While hikers walk by, blissfully unaware,
Of the furry brigade planning their fair share.

A chuckle erupts from a cheeky old crow,
Watching the summit's shenanigans flow.
With a wink and a caw, he joins in the fun,
Adding his two cents, 'This is just the begun!'

The summit may seem so silent and still,
But under the surface, there's raucous thrill.
A cacophony blooms as the sun sets low,
In this sneaky high place, where secrets overflow!

Voices of the Verdant

In the lands lush and oh so green,
The plants have a gossip, sprightly and keen.
Each leaf is a whisper, each stem a loud cheer,
As the daisies recount the latest dear.

The ferns sway with elegance, sharing their tales,
While the daisies giggle, tickling their scales.
The sunflowers nod, with heads held so high,
'Did you hear about the cat that learned how to fly?'

Laughter rings out from the buzzing bees,
As they drop juicy rumors with fluttered ease.
'Have you spotted the llama that leaps with delight?
He dances through daisies, such a curious sight!'

Amidst trees that chuckle and grasses that wink,
Nature's own sitcom is closer than you think.
Join in the chorus, let your laughter be heard,
In the garden of giggles, life's a funny word!

Mysterious Trails of Growth

Through winding paths where mushrooms glow,
Adventures await, as quick as a throw.
The acorns debate on who'll grow the most,
While snails on the sidelines cheer them, engrossed.

A glance from the mushrooms sparks wild intrigue,
Their patterns tell stories that dance and fatigue.
'Have you heard about Fern, who's plotting a spree?
She's planning a party—bring plant friends and tea!'

The vines stretch and tangle, forming a maze,
Where critters get lost in the laughter and craze.
A rabbit in slippers hops past with delight,
Making puns about carrots by the soft moonlight.

In this dance of green, where secrets unfold,
Each leaf has a laughter, more precious than gold.
Nature's own humor, a whimsy-filled show,
In trails that keep twisting, just let it all flow!

Timeless Tales of Tree Rings

Once a tree told a joke so tall,
It made squirrels giggle and owls enthrall.
Each ring held secrets, both funny and clever,
Like the time it wore a hat made of leather.

The woodpecker laughed, "I've heard it all!"
While the ants danced below, having a ball.
In the heart of the forest, humor takes flight,
Where trees whisper tales under moonlight.

Branches stretched wide as they shared a grin,
With the sun shining bright, letting laughter in.
Saplings listened close, learning the lore,
Then cracked their own jokes, who could ask for more?

In this leafy theater, the audience swayed,
A root was the drummer, a leaf serenade.
For each twist of bark and each ring so round,
Is a story of laughter eternally found.

Twilight Among the Pines

Under bending branches, a party so fine,
The pines are waltzing, sipping sweet brine.
A firefly's glowing, it tells a great pun,
"Why did the pine cone run? Just for fun!"

The critters convened, with a goblet of dew,
Chirping and chattering, all joyful and true.
The porcupine joked, "I'm in a prickly mood!"
Everyone howled; it was laughter brewed.

As the moon rose high, shadows danced on the ground,
Pines whispered secrets; silliness abound.
"Let's branch out tonight!" one pine did declare,
While the owls hooted, as if they were there.

And if trunks could giggle and roots could break dance,
The humor in nature would put you in a trance.
In twilight's soft glow, find joy in the trees,
For laughter's the language of the wildest leaves.

Nature's Echo Chamber

Once in a grove, an echo did shout,
"Did you hear the one about the wind, that's been out?"
It tickled the leaves and made the creek chuckle,
Even rocks couldn't help but give a soft huddle.

Every shout that rang bounced in delight,
From the tallest old oak to the shyest of sights.
"Why are trees such terrible secret keepers?"
"They always leaf you hanging—what are their deepers?"

The more they spoke, the more giggles grew loud,
Where the frogs sang along; they were quite proud.
Even shadows joined in with a dance on the floor,
As the echo repeated each joke evermore.

Nature's own theater, with laughter as art,
An echo chamber that warms every heart.
So the next time you ponder the whispers of woods,
Remember the giggles, life's jovial goods.

The Heartfelt Rumble of Roots

Deep down below, where the roots intertwine,
A party was brewing, oh, what a design!
"Why did the root cross the path?" asked one,
"To dig deeper in laughter, oh what fun!"

They curled and they twirled, with giggles astir,
Planting puns in the soil, what a humorous blur!
The worms joined in, wormed their way near,
With jokes from the depths, it was quite the cheer.

"Roses are red, violets are a riot,
In this tangled arena, who says we can't try it?"
Roots rumbled and tumbled, they tickled the dirt,
In this underground giggle, no one felt hurt.

So if you wander above without a care,
Know below in the soil, humor's everywhere.
With each heartfelt rumble, a giggle's in tow,
The roots hold the laughter, let the good times flow.

The Language of Needles

Whispering winds through branches sway,
Needles giggle in their playful way.
A squirrel stutters, chasing his tail,
While pine cones drop, like seeds of a tale.

Eavesdropping birds practice their tunes,
As the trees gossip under the moon.
They spill secrets with rustles and sways,
And chuckle at the sun's lazy rays.

Rabbits debate by the mossy rocks,
While ladybugs waltz on neighboring blocks.
The foliage dances, a whimsical sight,
As branches engage in a merry flight.

In this forest, joy brings a grin,
Nature's jesters, where laughter begins.
A punchline blossoms, and echoes persist,
In the realm of the needles, where none can resist.

Memories in the Mist

Among the fog, old jokes take flight,
With shadows prancing out of sight.
The morning dew, a slippery tease,
As squirrels leap with effortless ease.

Frogs croak rhymes in their own silly way,
While the mist shares tales of yesterday.
Whirling whippets, the wind starts to race,
And giggles are hidden in every trace.

A friendly owl hoots a comic refrain,
While misty mushrooms join in the fun chain.
They dance and sway with foliage bright,
Turning memory lapses into sheer delight.

Each twist and turn adds to the bliss,
In a world where laughter you never miss.
The mist rolls on, with giggles that last,
In this enchanted wood, ran wild and fast.

Hidden in the Horizon

Beneath the bowers, where sunlight's cast,
Lies a realm where hilarity's amassed.
The horizon peeks with a cheeky grin,
As shadows gesture, inviting in.

Frolicsome ferns, with fronds that sway,
Trade funny glances at the end of day.
The hills chuckle, rolling far and wide,
While whispers of whimsy take each stride.

Giggly gullies, where trickster streams flow,
With splashes of laughter, putting on a show.
As the sun dips low, creating a scene,
Where humor blooms in a meadow of green.

The horizon holds secrets, quirks in its fold,
Tales of tomfoolery, waiting to be told.
With every sunset painting the sky,
Fun memories linger, fluttering by.

Pinespeak

In the heart of the woods, trees stand tall,
Whispering nonsense that beckons us all.
A pine speaks softly, a riddle, a quirk,
Inviting us into their whimsical work.

The branches chuckle, the bark starts to laugh,
Saying "Come join us for a silly giraffe!"
With every crack of their needle-like grin,
They beckon the critters for a wild spin.

Fungi gather for the comedy show,
As the moss-topped rocks join in for a throw.
A raccoon roasts jokes over simmering pine,
While fireflies twinkle, feeling just fine.

From tree to tree, the laughter flows,
Creating a symphony only forest knows.
So listen carefully, join in the fun,
Pinespeak is magic under the sun.

Beneath the Arboreal Veil

Under branches twisted tight,
Squirrels debate who's most spry.
Whispers of winds with a teasing bite,
As they giggle, oh my, oh my!

Mossy carpets, comfy and green,
What's hiding there? A mossy scene!
Owl's eye rolls at the antics seen,
Nature's jesters in a leafy routine.

Chipmunks dance without a care,
Worms slide by unaware of the flair.
The tall trees laugh while swaying in air,
Invisible pranks beyond compare!

So join the fun beneath the shade,
Where every creature has a trade.
In this leafy world, joy is made,
And all secrets are simply displayed.

The Canopy's Cryptic Chorus

In the treetops, a songbird croons,
Jokes that tickle the afternoon.
Branches sway to a wispy tune,
While critters plot under the moon.

A raccoon dressed in dapper style,
Tips his hat with a cheeky smile.
Forest fashion, oh such a trial,
Each twig becomes a runway aisle.

Beneath bright leaves, shadows play tricks,
Where laughter simmers, a bubbling mix.
Nature's punchlines in the matrix,
The trees shake hands with all their wicks.

Join in the dance, let spirits soar,
Discover laughter, forevermore.
In the green, the heart will explore,
Each twig a tale, each leaf a roar!

Nature's Quiet Revelations

Beside the brook, whispers arise,
The stones chuckle, oh what a surprise!
A fish jumps up, maybe it flies,
In this world, everyone tries!

The bushes giggle as insects twirl,
With each soft buzz, they unfurl.
Flowers wink, the petals swirl,
In this green jungle, oddities whirl.

A jumping frog starts to complain,
"Why is it wet? I'll go insane!"
Nature's humor in every plane,
Makes the forest a light-hearted chain.

So listen closely to the trees,
They share their jokes with the breeze.
Laughter lingers among the leaves,
In this realm, everyone believes!

Footprints in the Forest's Memory

Footprints lead through leafy trails,
Where many a critter tells their tales.
The ground giggles at secret scales,
   Ticklish roots in nature's gales.

A rabbit hops, and what a sight!
Chasing shadows, full of delight.
Laughter echoes through day and night,
   A merry dance, purely alight.

The leaves murmur of the day's spree,
   As ants march with utmost esprit.
They've a party, quite the jubilee,
Beneath the boughs of an ancient tree.

So take a step where joy will lead,
   Surrender to laughter's joyful seed.
In the forest, all hearts are freed,
Where every moment plants a new deed!

Whispers of the Evergreen

In the forest where trees gossip,
Laughter rustles in every leaf.
Squirrels plotting their next heist,
Acorns dropped cause quite the grief.

Raccoons wear masks, oh so sly,
Stealing snacks right from the bags.
While owls roll their eyes nearby,
As the sap drips from old tags.

The pines giggle under the sun,
While branches stretch like lazy cats.
A secret party has begun,
With woodland critters and their hats!

The wind hums tunes of joy and cheer,
While the forest shakes with mirth.
It's a place of laughter, never fear,
Where the trees know what it's worth.

Shadows Beneath the Canopy

In the shade where giggles grow,
Shadow puppets dance in play.
A squirrel tells a tale, you know,
About a cat who lost her way.

The branches sway and spin around,
As raccoons tap-dance on the ground.
A deer attempts a wobbly twirl,
And every leaf begins to swirl.

But watch the fox with cunning eyes,
He's stealing pies baked by the wise.
"Who brought the cake?" a crow demands,
"Not me!" cries out the fox with hands.

As fireflies blink, the night unfolds,
Nature's stage, where laughter molds.
Underneath the twinkling skies,
Whispers of humor surely rise.

The Ancient Boughs' Confession

Two oak trees share secrets old,
About silly pranks from years ago.
One pulled a trick, so bold,
Dropping acorns on heads below.

"Remember that time?" one tree said,
"When we made the squirrels chase their tails?"
"Or how the rabbit jumped in dread,
When a breeze sent him on flailing trails?"

Ancient boughs creak with laughter,
As woodpeckers join the chatter.
What a sight, the forest's rafter,
With tales of joy that truly matter!

As dusk descends with a cheeky grin,
The branches sway, let the night begin.
A confession, a nod, a timer's spin,
In laughter's embrace, all lives in kin.

Veils of the Whispering Woods

In the woods where giggles hide,
Mossy carpets hide the jokes.
Chirping crickets, side by side,
Share punchlines with the froggy folks.

A raccoon peeks from behind the bark,
With mischief written on his face.
The trees sway, a joyous lark,
As they cheer for the playful race.

"Why did the tree refuse to play?
Because it couldn't find its roots!"
Echoes of laughter on display,
With nature's pulse in funny hoots.

Under veils of green so bright,
The forest breathes in pure delight.
With every giggle, every sight,
The woods prepare for endless night.

Lullabies of the Woodland

In the forest, whispers soar,
Squirrels giggle, wanting more.
Underneath the leafy bed,
A raccoon dreams of cheese instead.

Fireflies dance, a sparkling show,
As owls hoot, and crickets grow.
Nature sings a cheery tune,
While frogs croak 'Don't forget the moon!'

Bunnies bounce with comical grace,
Chasing shadows, a bumbling race.
When the sun sets, tales unfold,
Of topsy-turvy nights retold.

Rituals of the Old Growth

The gnarled trees wear hats of moss,
Hosting meetings, hoping to toss.
Squirrels debate on nutty matters,
While owls judge, they sure can patter.

A chorus of chirps fills the air,
With toads croaking without a care.
Branches sway like a lively dance,
Tree knots giggle at their own chance.

Mice share secrets, tucked in each nook,
While fireflies scribble in a book.
Evergreens chuckle, whisper and sway,
In the woods where wild things play.

Where the Shadows Play

In the thicket, shadows wander,
As chubby bats begin to ponder.
A hedgehog snorts, a sprightly friend,
Through the night, their giggles blend.

Moonlight paints the ground like cream,
As animals plot and scheme.
Puppies chase their own long tails,
While cats plot on tiny trails.

The owls hoot with luck and glee,
As ants march on to a wild spree.
Where shadows frolic, joy's the key,
In every nook, a mystery.

Nature's Quiet Chronicles

Upon the breeze, tales softly drift,
Of froggy leaps and the cat's gift.
Rabbits tell wild stories bright,
Of sock puppet plays in the moonlight.

Leaves turn pages with every gust,
Mice recite tales, a must!
Behind each tree, surprises lie,
A laughing breeze and a dreamy sigh.

The tall grass sways, bows low with grace,
As fireflies wink, lighting the place.
In the quiet woods, smiles ignite,
With whimsical wonders dancing at night.

Secrets Woven in Wood

In the forest, whispers play,
Trees tell tales in a funny way.
Squirrels giggle, hidden all day,
While birds make plans for a grand buffet.

A raccoon wears a clever disguise,
Cheeking acorns as he spies.
"Who will notice?" he slyly replies,
While a wise owl rolls his eyes high.

Here the roots wriggle in glee,
As branches dance, wild and free.
"Let's prank the winds," they decree,
"Who knew trees could be so cheeky?"

Nature chuckles in leafy delight,
With secrets shared under the moonlight.
If you listen closely, with all your might,
You might catch laughter, pure and bright.

The Lure of the Lesser Known

Among the quiet, there's a tease,
Hidden jokes in rustling leaves.
In shadows lurk the puzzled bees,
Trying to solve mysteries with ease.

The mushroom's cap is a top hat fine,
A dapper fungus—oh, how divine!
He tips it low, feeling quite benign,
"Join my laughter, or sip some wine!"

The little creek makes silly sounds,
Giggling stones as it bounds.
"Jump in quick, before we're found!"
The fish all smirk in water grounds.

A playful breeze will twist and twirl,
With all the secrets it can unfurl.
The hidden jokes in nature whirl,
As life lingers, an endless pearl.

Between the Twigs

We find small tales in twigs so thin,
Where ants host parties with a cheeky grin.
They offer crumbs with a flourish and spin,
While the spiders sneak in for a win.

In the night, the owls hoot loud,
Mixed with chuckles from the cloud.
"Is that a joke? I'm not so proud,"
Said the moon, wrapped in a misty shroud.

Between the branches, a dance unfolds,
Of critters young and stories old.
"Hey, did you hear? I'm feeling bold!"
Said the shy hedgehog, full of gold.

And as the daylight starts to creep,
The secrets shared, the fun to keep.
A world alive, in laughter deep,
In nature's heart, where we leap.

The Folklore of Fern

Beneath the ferns, there's humor bright,
Where fairies giggle at the sight.
They trade tall tales in moonlight,
With shadows moving, just out of sight.

An adventurous snail with a plan so grand,
Sets off on a journey across the land.
"Don't slow me down!" he waves his hand,
As bunnies laugh in a playful band.

The dew drops sparkle with a wink,
While the wise old toad begins to think.
"What's the punchline? Oh, do not blink!"
He croaks out riddles, making you think.

The forest thrives on silly trades,
With nature's laughter that never fades.
In every rustle and leafy cascade,
A tale of whimsy forever invades.

The Interview at Dusk

In the twilight's playful glow,
Trees chat and giggle, you know.
A squirrel in a suit, what a sight!
Checking his watch, feeling quite uptight.

A leaf rustles, a branch leans near,
Interview questions, oh dear, oh dear!
"What's your greatest strength, do you say?"
"To drop acorns and clear the way."

The sun blushes, the light turns shy,
A raccoon sneezes, oh my, oh my!
"Can you handle stress?" asks the wise owl,
"I can hoot and hoard, hear my growl!"

The dusk fades, laughter lingers still,
Job offers and jokes, what a thrill!
As the stars twinkle in the dark,
The forest resumes, with its gentle spark.

Wind-Kissed Chronicles

In a puff of wind, tales take flight,
Branches shimmy, a comical sight.
Whispers tickle the leaves so bright,
As the trees giggle, what pure delight!

A squirrel spins tales of nuts so grand,
Imitating acorn victory plans.
The breeze carries chuckles, playful and free,
As pine cones revolve like a wild jubilee!

Old roots gossip, stretching with ease,
"Did you hear about the bee in the breeze?"
Laughter erupts through the ancient wood,
Sharing the joy, it's all understood.

As night falls softly, shadows dance,
In the moonlight, we find our chance.
Each gust a giggle, each rustle a cheer,
Wind-kissed chronicles that bring us near.

Aromas of the Ancient Grove

In the heart of the grove, scents fly high,
Pineapple and cedar, oh my, oh my!
Old sap tales swirl, all fragrant and bright,
The trees crack jokes in the cool moonlight.

A raccoon in a chef hat arrives with flair,
Stirring up laughter with quite the rare air.
"What's cooking?" asks a wise old crow,
"Just a pinch of mischief and laughter to show!"

"Here's a dish served with humor from roots,
Sprinkled with giggles and acorn shoots."
The mushrooms chuckle, their caps all aglow,
As aromas of fun in the night flow.

Short trees tease tall ones, they wiggle and sway,
"Why so serious? Let's dance and play!"
And so they twirl in the moon's gentle beam,
Creating a feast of a whimsical dream.

Shadows Speak Among Pines

In the shadowy pines, whispers do swirl,
Branches trading secrets in twirls and twirls.
A shadow quips, "What a funny old tree!"
"I've seen more than you, just wait and see!"

The owls exchange winks, such wise little folks,
Plotting grand schemes through their chuckling strokes.
"What's your best joke?" asks the old sage,
"Why did the pine show up on stage?"

The answer erupts like a soft summer breeze,
"To branch out in laughter and bring us some ease!"
As shadows sway with a light-hearted grace,
A tapestry woven with fun, in this space.

The stars toss glimmers, while laughter erupts,
In the company of shadows, joyfully fluffed.
So let's raise a toast to the night's playful schemes,
Among pines, our laughter dances like dreams.

Beneath the Needle's Whisper

A squirrel wore glasses, quite out of style,
He read all the newspapers, with quite a smile.
The gossip of pines tickled his ears,
He chuckled alone, shaking off all his fears.

The branches were chatting, all twisted and bent,
About how the forest was once heaven-sent.
Fungi were huddled, in secrets they bet,
Who'd win the best prize for the weirdest haircut yet!

Woodland Reveries

The owls held a meeting, late into the night,
Debating who'd win a dance-off - quite a sight!
The raccoons brought snacks, all shiny and neat,
While the rabbits rolled dice, hoping for a treat.

Pine cones wore capes, just to join in the fun,
They fluttered and fumbled, all under the sun.
The moss made a joke, oh, it rattled the leaves,
And laughter erupted with rustles and heaves.

The Gentle Grasp of Twilight

As dusk painted shadows on trees oh-so-fine,
The crickets were crooning a mischievous line.
A firefly flickered, thinking he could sing,
But tripped on a twig - oh, what a silly thing!

The badger wore socks, mismatched and bright,
Declaring a contest for the funniest sight.
The hedgehog, quite nervous, hid under a leaf,
With dreams of his victory wrapped up in belief.

The Dance of the Leaf

Leaves twirled like ballerinas, high in the air,
Spinning and laughing without any care.
The wind played a flute, sweet melodies rang,
While nuts gathered round for an impromptu sang.

A chipmunk in tights sprung from branch to the ground,
He juggled with acorns, with grace all around.
The forest erupted - oh, what a delight!
With critters all giggling under the moonlight!

Starlight Through the Branches

Underneath the leafy sky,
A raccoon wears a bow tie.
He sips tea from a acorn cup,
Says, "Drink up, or you'll get stuck!"

The owls laugh with a hoot-hoot,
While squirrels dance in furry suits.
Moonlight winks through tangled vines,
As friendship flows through cosmic lines.

The Soul of the Timberline

A grumpy tree with dangling moss,
Complains that life is full of loss.
It's always stuck, can't go for a jog,
While rabbits prance and chase a fog.

The woodpecker drums a silly beat,
While ants march by, they do not cheat.
"Just sway and laugh," the branches shout,
"Be it rain or sunny clout!"

Mysteries in the Woodlands

In the woods where shadows play,
A rabbit runs in disarray.
"Why are you hopping here?" they tease,
"Chasing after honeybees!"

The frogs croak jokes that never land,
While lizards form a rock band.
Whispers float on breezy trails,
As the critters swap their tales.

Veins of the Vibrant

A tree with arms begins to dance,
While bushes giggle at a glance.
The sun brings warmth, but what a show—
A caterpillar wearing a tutu, oh!

The paths are wild with chirps and squeaks,
As wise old toads share silly peaks.
"Come join us in this leafy game,"
The forest shouts, "You'll never be the same!"

www.ingramcontent.com/pod-product-compliance
Lightning Source LLC
Chambersburg PA
CBHW071847160426
43209CB00003B/450